For Sterling and Heidi,
who rafted the Yampa and Green with us,
sharing our adventures one more time.
And for Farthen and Frodi,
wherever you are!

Powell's Book

INTRODUCTION

May 24, 1869, dawned bright and clear at Green River Station, Wyoming Territory. Four wooden boats, the *Emma Dean*, *Kitty Clyde's Sister*, *No Name*, and *Maid of the Canyon*, tugged on their ropes. The sturdy boats seemed as eager as the ten hardy men aboard them to set forth on their journey.

Where were they going? Their destination was to ride the Colorado River through the Grand Canyon, something no white person had done before . . . and lived to tell the tale. Their one-armed leader, Major John Wesley Powell, was determined to be the first to explore the vast canyon, or die trying.

The first part of the voyage would be spent exploring the canyons and riding the rapids and swift waters of the Green River. It would be almost two months before the explorers would reach its junction with the Grand River. Here, where the two rivers merged to form the Colorado, Powell and his men would begin to make history.

John Wesley Powell was well suited to lead such an expedition. As a curious boy in New York he had wandered fields and streams, observing nature and collecting arrowheads and plants. He grew up to become a geologist, a scientist who studies rocks to learn about the earth and its history. During the Civil War, Powell fought for the Union and lost his right arm to a bullet. Later, he decided to pursue his interest in the people and places of the great American West.

Before making his famous expedition, Powell had visited the region several times, accompanied by his wife, Emma, and several students. Most of the mountains, rivers, valleys, and deserts of the West had already been mapped. Only one large blank space remained: the great canyon that stretched nearly three hundred miles across northwestern Arizona. Powell, as it turned out, would not only be the first white man to explore and map it—he would name it as well.

Who were the nine brave men who accompanied Major Powell? There were four former soldiers: Captain Walter Powell (the major's brother), George Bradley, Seneca Howland, and Billy Hawkins. Joining them was Frank Goodman, a rich, adventurous Englishman, and Billy Dunn, a trapper and ox driver. Oramel Howland, a printer and Seneca's brother, Jack

Sumner, a trader, and Andrew Hall, a nineteen-year-old hunter and scout, completed the group.

The four rowboats were loaded with scientific instruments (compasses, barometers, thermometers, chronometers, and sextants), clothes, guns and ammunition, tools, traps, and enough food to last ten months. The boats had been designed by the major and built in Chicago especially for the expedition. They had been transported by train to the Green River crossing. The three longest vessels, each 21 feet, were made of strong oak to resist the battering of the rocks and waves. The fourth, at 16 feet, was constructed of pine so as to be fast and light enough to scout out dangers ahead on the river. Powell named this boat, the one in which he rode, the *Emma Dean*, in honor of his wife.

In general, the boats kept a certain order: the *Emma Dean*, under Powell's guidance, took the lead. Jack Sumner and Billy Dunn were his boatmen. Billy was also the expedition's cook. They steered and paddled while Powell gave directions. The major, unable to row because he had only one arm, sat in his chair lashed to the boat.

Kitty Clyde's Sister, with Captain Walter Powell and George Bradley, followed. *No Name* came

THE FOUR ROWBOATS WERE LOADED WITH SCIENTIFIC INSTRUMENTS,
CLOTHES, GUNS, TOOLS, TRAPS, AND ENOUGH FOOD TO LAST TEN MONTHS.

next, crewed by the Howland brothers and Frank Goodman. Last in line came the *Maid of the Canyon* with Billy Hawkins and Andrew Hall.

All the boats were divided into watertight compartments so that, in case of accident, not everything on board would be lost or ruined. The flour, meat, and other foods were split into thirds and placed on the heavier boats. Unloaded, the vessels were light enough to be carried by four men each when they reached rapids and waterfalls too dangerous to ride over.

As they set out on the Green River, Major Powell and his men, inexperienced sailors, struggled to control their boats. Very quickly, they learned how to navigate the dangerous waters. They learned the best way to dodge a rock, where the rapids could be safely run, and what would be the best places to camp onshore.

To keep track of their adventures, misadventures, and discoveries, Major Powell kept a journal "on long and narrow strips of brown paper, which were gathered into little volumes and bound in leather in camp as they were completed."

Here, in Major John Wesley Powell's words, is their daring story.

To you—J. C. Sumner, William H. Dunn, W. H. Powell, G. Y. Bradley, O. G. Howland, Seneca Howland, Frank Goodman, W. R. Hawkins, and Andrew Hall—my noble and generous companions, dead and alive, I dedicate this book.

—J. W. Powell

We Set Out

The good people of Green River Station turned out to see us start. We raised our little flag, pushed the boats from shore, and the swift current carried us down.

Our boats were heavily loaded, and only with the utmost care was it possible to float in the rough river without shipping water. A mile below town we ran on to a sandbar. The men jumped into the stream and lightened the vessels so that they drifted over, and on we went.

In trying to avoid a rock, the crewmen on one of the boats broke an oar. Thus crippled, the vessel struck the rock. The current was swift and the boat was sent reeling and rocking. In the confusion two other oars were lost overboard, and the boatmen were quite discomfited, much to the amusement of the other members of the party. The oars were soon caught and the boat was once more borne down the stream.

During the afternoon we ran to a point where the river swept the foot of a cliff, and here we camped for the night. There remained two hours until sunset, so I climbed the cliff and walked among the strangely carved rocks.

Standing on a high point, I looked off in every direction over a vast landscape. The rocks and cliffs glittered in the evening sun. Clouds, mountains, snowy fields, forests, and rocklands blended into one grand view.

What dangers await us on the rivers, I wondered? Would the men and the boats be up to the challenge of the white water ahead? Would we conquer the great canyon? Or would the swift waters defeat us as they had done others?

May 25

We started early this morning and ran along at a good rate until we were brought up against a gravelly bar. All jumped out and helped the boats over by main strength. Then a rain came and the river and clouds conspired to give us a good drenching. Wet, chilled, and tired to exhaustion, we stopped at a cottonwood grove on the riverbank, built a huge fire, made coffee, and were soon refreshed and quite merry.

"All aboard!" and we ran down the river for a dozen miles. On the way we passed the mouth of Black's Fork, a dirty little stream. Just below its mouth we landed and camped for the night.

May 26

We glided downstream past strangely shaped cliffs and caught glimpses of mountains in the distance. Deer were startled from among the willows. Several wild geese, after a chase, were shot for dinner, our midday meal. After eating, we passed through a narrow canyon into a broad valley. Later we reached the foot of the Uinta Mountains and in a cold storm went into camp.

Here the Green River cuts its way south through the mountains, which trend east and west, forming a series of canyons. The first major canyon we were to explore now lay before us.

Before attempting to enter it, we measured its walls with our instruments and found them to be 1,200 feet high. The rocks were of bright vermilion color. We named this canyon Flaming Gorge. I added the name to my map. The first blank

The Grand Canyon

The Grand Canyon is one of the largest canyons in the world. It runs 277 miles through northwestern Arizona and varies in width from less than 1 mile to 18 miles. It is about 1 mile deep.

The Colorado River and the streams feeding it created the Grand Canyon as their waters, over millions of years, cut through layers of rocks. The rocks at the top of the canyon's South Rim are about 250 million years old. Those at the bottom, where the river flows, are about 1.7 billion years old. Traveling down through these rock layers is like traveling back in time.

For thousands of years, various Native American tribes lived in the Grand Canyon. Some native people still live there today. The first Europeans to gaze in wonder at the vast canyon were a group of Spanish soldiers. In 1540, while searching for gold, they reached the rim of the canyon. Seeing nothing of interest to them, they left without exploring farther.

Today, more than five million people from around the world visit the natural wonder to which Major Powell gave the name, the Grand Canyon.

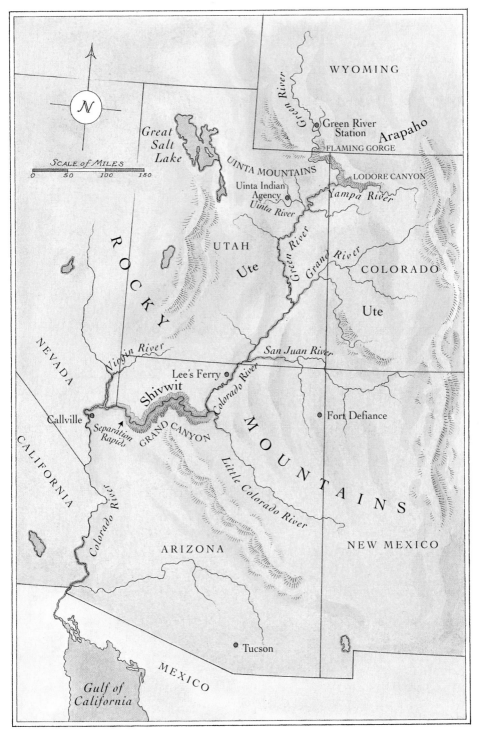

POWELL'S JOURNEY TO THE GRAND CANYON STARTED AT GREEN RIVER
STATION.

space was accurately filled.

The distance from Green River City to Flaming Gorge was 62 miles.

May 30

Today we ventured into Flaming Gorge. We began with some trepidation. Water filled the channel from cliff to cliff, plunging swiftly down among great rocks.

The old mountaineers had told us the canyon rapids could not be run. The Indians had warned, "Water catch them." But we were all eager for the trial, and off we went.

I stood up on the deck of my boat to seek a way among the wave-beaten rocks. Untried as we were with such waters, the moments were filled with intense anxiety.

Soon our boats reached the swift current. We threaded the narrow passage with exhilarating velocity, mounted the high waves, whose foaming crests dashed over us, and plunged into the troughs until we reached the quiet water below. Then came a feeling of great relief. Our first rapid was run!

From Flaming Gorge we entered a new

canyon. We named it Horseshoe Canyon for its shape, and on we went.

Later, we saw kingfishers playing about a small stream entering the river, so we adopted the names Kingfisher Creek, Kingfisher Park, and Kingfisher Canyon. More blank places were filled in on my map. We camped where Kingfisher Canyon met the river.

May 31

Today we started down another canyon and reached rapids made dangerous by high rocks lying in the channel. We could not safely ride the boats through such rough rapids so we went to shore. We unloaded the boats. Six men using ropes tied to the ends of the boats guided them one by one over the rapids. Then we carried our equipment along the shore to the boats.

In the afternoon we again came to dangerous rapids. We did the same work once more. As we encountered more such rapids, we frequently had to lower the boats with the ropes and portage our gear around the rapids. Such portages were tiring work for the men.

At the foot of a cliff we found a

portage
(POOR tij) to carry boats or goods overland around an obstacle such as rapids

long slope covered with pines. Under these we made our beds. The cliffs around us were of red sandstone and stretched 2,500 feet toward the heavens. As twilight deepened, the cliffs grew dark and somber. The threatening roar of the water was loud and constant. I lay awake with thoughts of tomorrow and the canyons to come.

June 1

Today we had an exciting ride. The river rolled down a canyon at a wonderful rate and we made almost railroad speed. The rocks pushed up great waves, which the boats leapt over like startled deer bounding through a forest. We ran twelve miles in an hour.

Then a distant roar was heard. Slowly approaching the point we came to a falls. We tied up just above them, unloaded the boats, and, using ropes, let the vessels down over the falls.

After portaging, the men were exhausted, so we camped for the night.

June 2

This morning we made a trail along the shore and transported the cargoes to below another waterfall. Then we let the boats over the fall and were ready to start before noon.

On a rock above our portaging path we noticed an inscription: Ashley 1855. James Baker, an old-time mountaineer, had once told me about a party of men starting down the river in round bull boats made of buffalo skin. Ashley was named as one of the men. His boat had been swamped and some men drowned.

The word *Ashley* was a warning to us, and we resolved on great caution. Ashley Falls was the name we gave to this cataract.

June 3

This morning we spread our rations, clothes, etc. on the ground to dry. Several men went hunting. I walked six miles and found a stand of pine trees. The grassy carpet was bedecked with crimson velvet flowers, set in clusters on pear-shaped cactus plants. Here and there little blue-eyed flowers peeped through the grass. The air was filled with fragrance. A mountain brook, ponded by beaver dams, ran through the midst.

Mule, deer, and elk abounded here. Grizzly bears were abundant. Here wild cats, wolverines,

THE GRASSY CARPET WAS BEDECKED WITH CRIMSON VELVET FLOWERS.
MULE, DEER, AND ELK ABOUNDED.

and mountain lions were at home. The forest was filled with the music of birds.

This was a quiet place from the raging waters of the canyons.

June 4

We started early.

Halfway down the valley, a spur of red mountain stretched on either side of the river. The rock walls were low, but vertical. A vast number of swallows had built their adobe houses on the face of the cliffs. The waters were deep and quiet, but the swallows were swift and noisy, sweeping by or chattering while their young ones clamored for food. They were a noisy people. We called this Swallow Canyon.

Down the river we glided until an early hour in the afternoon when we camped under a giant cottonwood tree. Our party killed wild ducks, and during the afternoon a mess of fish was taken.

June 5

Today Billy Dunn and I climbed a mountain to gauge our altitude. Two hours' hard work brought us to the summit. The nearby ridges were green with pine and cedar trees. To the west we gazed at snow-covered mountains. To the north we glimpsed the plains of the upper Green River through which we had traveled. The river, winding its way south, lay far below our feet.

We climbed down, reached camp tired and hungry, eager to talk about the glory of the landscape we had seen.

June 6

At daybreak I was awakened by a chorus of birds. It was as if all the feathered songsters of the region had come to the old cottonwood tree. Warblers, woodpeckers, and flickers sang above, meadowlarks sounded their notes in the grass, and wild geese honked on the river. A real morning concert for *me*.

Our cook had been an ox driver on one of those long wagon trains now no longer seen. But he hadn't forgotten his old ways. In the midst of my pleasant concert he shouted: "Roll out! Roll out! Bulls in the corral! Chain up the gaps! Roll out! Roll out!"

He was our breakfast bell this morning.

Today we passed easily down the river, for there were no rapids, and camped at the head of another canyon. A brief shower rained upon us.

June 7

We remained at this camp. This morning three of us climbed to the summit of a cliff above us and found its altitude to be 2,086 feet. The rocks were split with fissures, deep and narrow, sometimes running a hundred feet or more to the bottom. On one rock we found a pool of clear, cold water caught from yesterday evening's shower.

We walked to the edge of the cliff and stood on the brink of the canyon, looking down at the river below. I had never had difficulty doing this, but it had taken several years of mountain climbing to cool my nerves so that I could sit with my feet over the edge and calmly look down a precipice two thousand feet.

And yet I cannot look on and see another do the same.

When we returned to camp at noon, the sun shone in splendor on vermilion walls, shaded green and gray where the rocks were lichened over. The river filled the channel from wall to wall. Ahead, the canyon opened like a beautiful portal to a region of glory.

Later, as the sun was going down, shadows settled in the canyon. The vermilion gleams and roseate hues slowly changed to somber brown above. Black shadows crept over the cliffs below. Now the canyon was a dark portal to a region of gloom, the gateway through which we were to enter on our voyage of exploration tomorrow.

What shall we find? I wondered.

June 8

We entered the canyon and until noon found a succession of rapids over which our boats had to be taken.

Here I must further explain our method of proceeding at such places. The *Emma Dean* would go in advance, the other boats following in obedience to my signals. When approaching a rapid or waterfall, I would stand on deck to examine it. The oarsmen meanwhile would back water so that we would drift as slowly as possible.

If I saw a clear chute or passage between the

rocks, away we would go, with the other boats trailing us. Next we had to contend with the billowing waves. Caused by waterfalls and rapids, the waves plunged down ten or twenty feet, then sprang up again in a great surge. They continued billowing down and up until they gradually subsided into quieter waters below. The waves were always there below a fall, and we could count them.

A boat riding such waves leaps and plunges with great velocity. The difficulty is to avoid being capsized or washed overboard. If the boat strikes a wave the instant after it breaks, the mad breaker dashes its spray over the vessel and washes overboard all who do not cling tightly. If the boat chances to get caught in a side current, so as to strike the wave "broadside on," and the wave breaks at the same instant, the vessel is capsized. Then we must cling closely to her, for the water-tight compartments act as buoys, or floats. And we go madly along, dragged through the waves until the still waters are reached, when we right the boat and climb back onboard.

So much for running the rapids. If upon examining the waters I saw that the river channel was beset entirely across with rocks, I would signal the other boats to pull to land. I would then walk along the shore for a closer examination. If I could find no clear channel, the hard work of portaging would begin.

We portaged and rode the rapids today.

Tonight we camped on a little shelving rock between the river and the foot of the cliff. With night comes gloom into these great depths. We sat by our campfire, made of driftwood, and told stories of our "wild" lives. My men had seen many dangers in the mountains, on the plains, and on the battlefields of the South in the Civil War. It was late before we spread our blankets on the beach.

Lying down, I looked up between the towering canyon walls to see only a little crescent of sky with two or three constellations peering down upon us. I did not sleep for some time, as the excitement of the day had not worn off. Soon I saw a bright star that appeared to rest on the very verge of the cliff before floating over the canyon. It seemed at first like a jewel set in the rock and, as it moved out from the cliff, I almost wondered that it did not fall.

No Name No More

Andy Hall suggested we call this the Canyon of Lodore after the poem "The Cataract of Lodore," and the name was adopted. The rest of the men called the canyon the Gates of Hell.

Very slowly we made our way, often climbing on the rocks at the edge of the water for a few hundred yards to examine the river channel before running it.

Sometimes the water, smooth and unruffled, descended into a narrow, angry channel that spilled into a "pit" in the river. Great care had to be taken not to pass over the brink into one of these pits, for a boat could easily be overturned and the crew drowned.

Realizing such a pit lay ahead of us, I ordered my boat to shore. I walked along the bank, examining the river, leaving one man with a flag to guide the other boats to my landing place.

Seeing that the boat immediately following us made shore all right, I felt no more concern about the others trailing behind. But a minute after, I heard a shout.

The *No Name*, with the Howland brothers and Frank Goodman aboard, was shooting down the river straight into the center of the pit! I scrambled along, looking for the *No Name*, which had quickly disappeared.

The first fall I saw was only twelve feet high, and we had often easily run such. But below, the river tumbled down into a channel filled with treacherous rocks. The waves broke into whirlpools, beating the water into a fury of foam.

I passed a great crag to see the *No Name* strike a rock, rebound from the shock, careen, and fill with water. Two of the men lost their oars and could not control the boat. It swung around and was carried downstream broadside at a rapid rate. The boat struck another rock amidships, breaking in two. All three men were thrown into the river.

The larger part of the boat floated buoyantly. They seized it, and down the river they drifted to a second rapid filled with huge boulders. The boat hit again and was dashed to pieces. The men and fragments were quickly carried beyond my sight.

Running, I turned a bend and saw a man's head above water. It was Frank Goodman, clinging to a rock with a grip upon which his life depended. Coming opposite, I saw Oramel Howland going to his aid from an island upon which he had been washed. Howland came near enough to reach Goodman with a pole. Goodman let go of the rock, grasped the pole, and was pulled ashore. Seneca Howland, washed farther downstream, managed to safely land on the island.

This seems a long time as I tell it, but it was quickly done.

Now the three men were stranded on the island, with a swift, dangerous river on either side of them and a raging waterfall below. The *Emma Dean* was brought down, and Jack Sumner, starting above as far as possible, pushed out. Right skillfully he plied the oars, and with a few strokes, reached the men.

Then the men pulled the boat upstream until they stood in water up to their necks. One held the boat until the others had climbed in and were ready to pull. He gave the boat a push, grasped it with his hands, and hung on as the other men pulled for our shore.

We were as glad to shake hands with them as though they had been on a voyage around the world and had been wrecked on a distant coast.

Later, down the river half a mile, we found the cabin of the *No Name*. Ragged and splintered, it had floated against a rock and lay stranded. There were valuable articles in the cabin—one third of our supplies of rations, instruments, and clothing. But I determined that no life should be risked trying to save them. I had to accept the fact that the items were lost.

We camped for the night on the rocky shore. In all those dark hours, however, no sleep came to me. I was very troubled by our loss. Although we had anticipated accidents such as this one by dividing up our supplies among three boats, one third of our equipment and food was gone. What was worse, however, was the loss of all six of our barometers. We had started with duplicates of everything deemed necessary for success. But in the distribution, there was one exception to this precaution—the six barometers in their protective case had all been mistakenly placed in one boat.

Now they were lost!

There was a possibility that the barometers might still be in the cabin, for that was where they

Powell's Instruments

John Wesley Powell was a scientist and his expedition was primarily a scientific one. In order to measure altitude and determine direction and location, he used a variety of instruments.

Barometers, which measure the pressure of the atmosphere, were used to determine the altitude of the river, the falls, canyon walls, and the surrounding land. Thermometers kept track of the temperatures in the canyons. (Temperatures at the bottom of the Grand Canyon might be as much as 25 degrees Fahrenheit [14 degrees Celsius] higher than at the top.) Sextants established the expedition's location by measuring the height of the moon, sun, and planets above the horizon line. Chronometers kept accurate time, necessary to pinpoint the group's longitude. Compasses helped the party gauge the exact direction the twisting rivers were taking at any particular time.

All of the instruments were crucial to the success of the mission — mapping the canyons of the Colorado.

were kept. I knew I had to have them in order to measure the depth of the canyons through which we passed. Without such information, my maps would be incomplete and inaccurate.

But how to reach the barometers? Would they be there tomorrow or would the river shift the wreck? Would I be forced to climb out of the canyon and hike more than two hundred miles to Salt Lake City to obtain new ones?

June 10

I decided we had to risk retrieving the barometers from the wreck. After breakfast I went for another examination. The cabin had disappeared!

Then I saw it, carried fifty or sixty feet farther downstream. In its new position, I was satisfied it could now be reached safely.

Jack Sumner and Billy Dunn volunteered to make the attempt in the *Maid of the Canyon*. Steering skillfully, they reached the wreck, where they gingerly groped among the pieces of jagged, splintered wood. It was not long before they pulled out the barometer case. The boys set up a shout, and I joined them, pleased they should be as glad as myself to save the instruments.

But when Dunn and Sumner returned they brought more than just the barometers with them. To my surprise, they lifted up a three-gallon keg of whiskey! It was this discovery that had caused my men to put up such a shout.

It seems they had taken it aboard unbeknownst to me. Now I am glad they did, for it did them good, as they had been drenched every day by the cold water of the river.

Later we camped for the night farther down on the shore. While some of the men built a fire, a group of us, walking about, made a discovery. We found an iron bake oven, tin plates, part of a boat, and many other fragments. This, we realized, was the place where Ashley's party had been wrecked. Far upstream we had seen his name carved in the rock, yet knew not what had become of his party. The evidence scattered before us told of his ending.

We adopted the name Disaster Falls for the scene of so much peril and loss.

June 13

Rocks, rapids, and portages still. We camped on a patch of floodplain covered with a stand of box elders, stopping early in the day in order to spread the clothing and rations to dry. Everything was wet and spoiling.

We stayed here, resting and recovering for two days.

June 16

Late this afternoon we made a short run to the mouth of a little creek. Here we camped, with a group of cedars on one side and a dense mass of box elders and dead willows on the other.

I decided to make an exploration of the area and left camp to climb up the cliffside. While I was gone a whirlwind scattered our campfire among the long branches of the dead willows, causing a great conflagration. The fire raging wildly, my men rushed for the boats, leaving all they could not readily seize. They ran, their clothes afire, their hair singed. George Bradley's ears were scorched.

Billy Dunn, the cook, filled his arms with the mess kit. Jumping into a boat, he stumbled and fell. Away went our cooking utensils into the river. Our plates, spoons, knives, and forks—all gone!

The men cut loose the boats as flames, running

out on the overhanging willows, began to scorch the vessels. Once on the river, they encountered a rapid filled with rocks. On they shot, no channel explored, no signal to guide them!

I saw them, but from my position on the cliff above, I had not yet discovered the fire. The strange movements of the men filled me with astonishment. Down the rocks I clambered and ran to the bank. When I arrived, the boats had landed downstream, where I joined them and learned what had occurred.

We returned to camp to see if we could save anything. There was some clothing and bedding, also a few tin cups, basins, and a camp kettle. This was all the mess kit we now had.

Yet we did just as well as ever.

June 17

We ran downstream to the mouth of the gentle Yampa River where it joins the Green. So far this trip has been a chapter of disasters and toils, even beyond the power of pen to tell. The river's roar was heard unceasingly from the hour we entered the canyons until we landed here. No quiet in all that time. But the canyon walls and cliffs, peaks and crags, amphitheaters and alcoves told a story of beauty and grandeur that I hear yet—and shall ever hear.

The Yampa River enters the Green River from the east. Opposite the mouth of the Yampa towers a rock about seven hundred feet high and a mile long. Nearby, on the Yampa's right bank, lies a meadow large enough for a farm. Here we spent three days, making a series of astronomic observations for latitude and longitude.

We made another observation while we were here. We found that when we stood across from the great rock and spoke, our words were echoed back to us. They were repeated with a startling clearness and in a soft, mellow tone that transformed them into magical music. One could scarcely believe the extraordinary sound of the echo of his own voice. From some positions, two or three echoes came back. We named the place Echo Rock.

One afternoon George Bradley and I climbed some cliffs to the north. There, above us, stood a flock of mountain sheep. They eyed us intently. Their color was like the gray sandstone beneath them and, standing still, they appeared to be carved forms. Suddenly a ram beat a rock with

OPPOSITE THE MOUTH OF THE YAMPA RIVER TOWERS A ROCK ABOUT SEVEN HUNDRED FEET HIGH AND A MILE LONG.

his foot and, wheeling around, all the sheep bounded away together, leaping over rocks and climbing walls where no man could follow, and this with an ease and grace most wonderful.

A Narrow Escape

Desiring to climb Echo Rock to measure its altitude, Bradley and I hiked up a gulch. We walked along on a smooth rock bench next to the wall, then up again over broken rocks. We climbed until we had ascended eight hundred feet, when we were met by a sheer precipice. Looking about, we found a place where it seemed possible to climb.

I went ahead. We proceeded until we were nearly to the summit, where I gained a foothold and grasped a rock overhead. But then, I could go no farther up! I could not step back, for I dared not let go with my hand, and I could not reach a foothold below without doing so.

I called to Bradley for help. He found a way to the top of the rock over my head but could not reach me. He looked around for a stick or limb of a tree to have me hold, but he found none.

The moment was critical. Standing on my toes,

my muscles began to tremble. It was eighty feet to the foot of the precipice. If I lost my hold I would fall to the bottom and tumble still farther down the cliff.

It occurred to Bradley to take off his pants. He swung them down to me. I hugged close to the rock, let go with my hand and seized the dangling legs. With his assistance I gained the top.

I was saved!

We found an easy way down.

June 21

Back on the river, our party entered another canyon today. It was much narrower than any we had seen. The walls were high and vertical, and the river filled the whole space across. The Green was greatly increased in size and speed here by the Yampa. All of this water, confined in a narrow, rocky channel, was set eddying and spinning in whirlpools. The waters waltzed their way through the canyon, making their own rippling, roaring music.

We managed our boats with difficulty. They spun from side to side, and we knew not where we were going. It was impossible to keep the vessels headed down the stream. At first, this caused us great alarm, but we soon found there was little danger. It was the merry mood of the river to dance through this deep, dark gorge. Right gaily did we join in the sport.

June 22

Into the middle of the stream we rowed. Down the rapid river we glided, only making strokes enough to guide the boat. What a headlong ride it was! I was filled with an exhilaration experienced only once before in riding a fleet horse over the outstretched prairie.

One, two, three, four miles we went, rearing and plunging with the waves, until we wheeled to the right into a beautiful open grassland. Here the river, broad and deep, meandered, interrupted by many wooded islands. We landed on one and made camp. I named this lovely place Island Park and called the swirling canyon above Whirlpool Canyon.

June 23

We repaired our boats, which had had hard knocks and sprung leaks. Two men climbed the cliff at the foot of Whirlpool Canyon and measured the walls. Billy Hawkins went hunting on a nearby mountain. George Bradley and I spent the day among the rocks, studying an interesting geologic fold and collecting fossils. Late in the afternoon the hunter returned from the mountain, bringing a fine, fat deer. We gave his name to the mountain—Mount Hawkins.

June 24

Today Bradley and I climbed Mount Hawkins. We found its summit to be nearly three thousand feet above camp. It required some labor to scale it, but at the top, what a view! The river wheeled to the right at the foot of Whirlpool Canyon in a great curve through Island Park. At the lower end, the river cut into the mountain, creating a gorge that split the mountain ridge for six miles. All this we could see from where we stood on the summit of Mount Hawkins. We named the gorge Split Mountain Canyon.

June 25

Today we entered Split Mountain Canyon, sailing

through a broad, flaring brilliant gateway. We ran three rapids. Then we had a series of eight rapids over which we let the boats down with lines. This occupied the entire day. We camped at the mouth of a great cave, from which we could see far up-river. A line of crags bordered either side of the water, and Mount Hawkins rose in the distance.

June 26

This afternoon we found three falls in close succession. We landed, carried our rations over the rocks, and let our boats shoot the falls, checking and bringing them to land with lines in the eddies below. When we were once more on the river, we were carried down by the swift waters at great speed, shearing around rocks with timely strokes of our oars.

The canyon opened up into a beautiful valley and we camped under a grand old cottonwood tree. This evidently was a frequent resort for the Indians. Tent poles were lying about, and the dead embers of campfires were found. On the plains, antelope were feeding. Now and then we spotted a wolf. After dark the wolves made the air resound with their howling.

This morning, Andy Hall, Frank Goodman, Billy Hawkins, and I headed for the Uinta Indian Agency. It was a toilsome walk, twenty miles across a sand desert. We arrived at dusk. Captain Dodd, the agent, was away at Salt Lake City, but his assistants received us kindly. It was pleasant to see a house once more.

Indian Agencies

The U. S. government, in order to provide for Native Americans, built Indian agencies. These posts were scattered throughout the West. Their main function was to receive supplies from the government and give them to the Indians. Often there was also a trading post at the agency, where anyone could trade for supplies, receive and send mail, and meet travelers.

We Meet Chief Tsauwiat and His Wife

I went this morning to visit Chief Tsauwiat. He is more than one hundred years old. He had a pipe he used a long time. I offered to exchange with him and he seemed glad to accept.

The chief's wife exerts a great influence on these people and is much revered. She is the only Indian woman I ever knew to occupy a place in the council ring. She had much to say to me concerning the condition of her people, and seemed very anxious that they should learn to cultivate the soil, own farms, and live like white men.

I saw their farms in a very beautiful district, where many streams meandered across plains and meadows. A number of the Indians had each three acres, on which they raised wheat, potatoes, turnips, pumpkins, and other vegetables. The crops looked well.

The Indians still occupied lodges. They refused to build houses, saying that when anyone dies in a lodge it is always abandoned and, very often, burned with all of the effects of the deceased. Any houses that had been built for them had been treated in the same way.

Wandering about the little farms today, I saw the foundations of ancient buildings. The Indians, seeing that I was interested in these things, showed me other places where these evidences remained. They told me they knew nothing about the people who once dwelt here but that in the canyon nearby there are rocks covered with pictures made by "the ancient ones."

July 5

Frank Goodman, our English companion, whose boat had been lost and with it his clothes, informed me this morning that he had decided not to go on with the party. He said he had seen danger enough. Since our remaining three crafts were heavily loaded, I was content he should leave. He had been a faithful man.

We started early on our return to the boats, proceeding on horseback with two Indians, who

Native Americans and the Grand Canyon

For more than eight thousand years Native Americans have lived in the Grand Canyon, attracted to the rich, fertile soil found in the region. Then, as now, water for crops was a problem. If the rains came, crops flourished. If they failed, so did the corn, squash, and beans needed for survival. Water could be carried from the rivers to irrigate the fields, but it would not be sufficient to support a large number of people in any one area.

Native Americans reached the bottom of the canyon through several breaks in the tall walls. Today most of the Indians are gone, although some members of the Havasupai tribe still live in parts of the canyon.

Throughout the area, as well as in other places in the Southwest, the native peoples left behind works of art on the surfaces of rocks. Many rock art pictures are of animals: deer, roadrunners, lizards, antelope, and birds. Others are of humans. Some show gods or unusual events, such as an eclipse or a shower of shooting stars. The native peoples created these pictures either by patiently etching, or chipping into, the stone or by painting directly on it.

were to bring the animals back.

We gave this valley, where we have camped these days and which abounds in antelope, the Indian name Won'sits Yuav — Antelope Valley.

July 7

We found quiet water today, the river sweeping in great and beautiful curves, the canyon walls steadily increasing in altitude. Late in the afternoon we found the river very much rougher and came upon rapids, not dangerous, but still demanding close attention. We camped on the right bank, having made twenty-six miles.

July 11

We ran a rapid, and in doing so broke an oar, and then lost another. Now the *Emma Dean* had but two oars. We saw no wood from which new oars could be made.

We approached another rapid. Standing on deck, I thought it could be run, and on we went. Coming nearer, I saw the waters piled against the cliff. We shot by a big rock. A wave rolled over our little boat and filled her. The place was too dangerous and I waved my red flag signaling to the others to land wherever they could.

Another wave rolled the *Emma Dean* over, throwing me into the river. I found swimming was very easy. I had only to ply strokes to keep my head out of the water. When a breaker rolled over me, I closed my mouth and was carried through it. The boat drifted ahead of me. I overtook her and found Sumner and Dunn clinging to her.

We landed to find we had lost our guns, a barometer, and two blankets, all of which were in the open compartment when we went over.

We built a huge fire and spread our clothing out to dry. From some driftwood we selected logs to make new oars, for ours were all lost. The remainder of the day was spent sawing out new oars. The men found this a difficult task.

July 12

This morning the oars were finished and we set forth again. Passed several bad rapids and then we came to a fall and decided to run it. The *Emma Dean* made it over all right.

The *Kitty Clyde's Sister*, with George Bradley

and Captain Powell aboard, was carried into great waves where she was tossed about. Suddenly, Bradley was knocked over the side. However, his foot caught under the seat, and he was dragged along in the water with his head down. He grasped the gunwale with his left hand and lifted his head above the water now and then to get a breath.

My brother pulled with all his power for half a dozen strokes until the danger was past. Then he seized Bradley and pulled him in.

The men in the *Maid of the Canyon* above, seeing the danger, paddled to shore and let their boat down by lines through the falls.

Just here we emerged from the Canyon of Desolation, as we had named it, into a more open country, which extended for nearly a mile. Then we entered another canyon, Gray Canyon we called it, for it cut through gray sandstone.

Tonight we camped on a sand beach. The wind blew a hurricane and the drifting sand almost blinded us. Nowhere could we find shelter. The wind blew all night. The sand sifted through our blankets and piled over us until we were as covered as in a snowdrift. We were glad when morning came and this horrible wind died.

July 13

We had an exhilarating ride. The river was swift, and there were many smooth rapids. I stood on deck, keeping careful watch ahead as we glided along, mile after mile. We emerged from Gray Canyon and camped under a cottonwood tree.

July 15

There was an exquisite charm in our ride today down a beautiful canyon that grew deeper with every mile. Its walls were curved and grandly arched and they were reflected in the quiet waters in many places. We were all in fine spirits. We would whistle or discharge a gun in order that we might listen to the echoes among the cliffs. We named this place Labyrinth Canyon.

July 16

We went our winding way.

The Colorado at Last

July 17

In many places the walls were overhanging on
either side. The stream was quiet, and we glided
along through a strange, weird, grand region.
The landscape was rock—cliffs of rock, tables of
rock, plateaus of rock, terraces of rock, crags
of rock—ten thousand strangely carved forms.
Rocks everywhere and no vegetation, no soil, no
sand. In long, gentle curves the river wound
about these rocks.

Late in the afternoon the water became swift
and our boats made great speed. An hour of this
rapid running brought us to the junction of the
Grand River and Green River at the foot of Still-
water Canyon. Here these waterways united in
the solemn depths, more than twelve hundred
feet below the surface of the country, to form
the mighty Colorado River.

THE LANDSCAPE WAS ROCK—CLIFFS OF ROCK, TABLES OF ROCK, PLATEAUS OF ROCK, TERRACES OF ROCK, CRAGS OF ROCK—TEN THOUSAND STRANGELY CARVED FORMS.

The Colorado River

The Colorado River begins high in the Rocky Mountains of Colorado, winds its way down 1,360 miles through the states of Colorado, Utah, Arizona, and California, and continues for 90 miles in Mexico before emptying into the Gulf of California. It has always been a vital source of water for farmers and ranchers in the West. The Colorado is the most important river of the Southwest, and one of the most fought-over waterways in the world.

July 18

The day was spent drying our rations, which were badly injured. The flour had been wet and dried so many times it was all musty and full of hard lumps. We made a sieve of mosquito netting and ran our flour through it, losing more than two hundred pounds. Our losses, by the wrecking of the *No Name*, and by various mishaps since, together with the amount thrown away today, left us little more than two months' worth of supplies.

To make them last until we reached our goal, we
would have to be fortunate to lose no more. I
knew not how many miles that would be.

Our boats needed attention, too. We turned
them over, repaired broken boards with pieces of
driftwood, and filled cracks with pine pitch that
I collected. We put everything in the best shape
possible for the vigorous campaign ahead.

July 21

This morning we started down the Colorado. It
would not be long before we would enter the
Grand Canyon. The river here was rough with
bad rapids. Two very hard portages were made.
In running a rapid, the *Emma Dean* was
swamped. Bradley, Dunn, and I were thrown
into the river. We clung to the boat, and in the
quiet water below she was righted and bailed
out. Our party camped on the rocks and scarcely
found room to lie down.

July 23

Difficult rapids and falls, in many places more
abrupt than in any canyons through which we had

passed. We named this place Cataract Canyon.

Our way was through a gorge, grand beyond description. The walls were nearly vertical, the river broad and swift, but free from rocks and falls. From the surface of the water to the brink of the cliffs was eighteen hundred feet. At this great depth the river rolled in solemn majesty. We seemed to be in the very bowels of the earth. Yet I know we must go deeper still before our journey's end.

The afternoon and evening were spent discussing the probabilities of successfully navigating the river. The conclusion was there were great descents yet to be made, but if they were in rapids and short falls, as they had been, we should be able to overcome them. All the men seemed to be in agreement, but I noticed the look shared by the Howland brothers. Did they really agree?

How will it be in the future? I worried.

July 24

We made three long, hard portages, the water tumbling down among rocks and chutes. We stopped for the night only three fourths of a mile below the last camp. A very hard day's work had been done.

The men grumbled, hungry, tired, fearful of the unknown river ahead. My brother sang and helped lift their spirits a little.

I looked at the water and listened to its roar. Hours ago, deep shadows had settled into the canyon as the sun passed behind the cliffs. Now the sun had gone down. Darkness was upon us. But the waves rolled with crests of foam so white they gave off a light of their own. The water heaped up in mounds and cones. Where rocks came near the surface, the water formed a chute above, struck, and shot up fifteen feet. Then it piled back in gentle curves, as in a fountain. And on and on the river tumbled and rolled.

Two months have passed since our voyage of discovery began.

July 29

We entered a canyon today with low, red walls. There we found the ruins of an ancient three-story building with walls of stone. The lower story was almost intact. On the face of the cliff, under the building and along the river for three hundred yards, there were many etchings. I am determined to learn more of these old ones someday. Now we must think only of leaving our canyon of captivity.

July 30

We made good progress today, as the water, though smooth, was swift. The men joked more, which pleased me. If only we had food, especially fresh meat, to eat. Apples, biscuits with lumpy flour, and coffee gave us not the strength we needed to overcome the obstacles before us.

July 31

We had a cool, pleasant ride today. We discovered the mouth of the San Juan River, where we camped. The afternoon was given to seeking some way by which we could climb out of the canyon, but we could see no way out from here.

Will all the men finish the journey with me? Or will some leave and look for a way out by climbing?

August 3

On the walls, and back many miles into the country, were numerous buttes. They presented a curious ensemble of wonderful features —

carved walls, royal arches, glens, alcove gulches, mounds, and monuments.

From which of these features should we select a name? We decided to call the canyon Glen Canyon.

August 5

With anxiety we entered a narrow canyon with vertical walls. More rapids and falls. We came to a drop of sixteen feet, around which we portaged. Then a run of two miles, and another portage, long and difficult. Weary, we camped on a bank of sand.

August 7

We were to have an eclipse of the sun today. Captain Powell and myself left early, taking our instruments to observe the eclipse. After four hours' hard climbing we reached twenty-three hundred feet and quietly waited for the eclipse. But clouds came on and rain fell, and sun and moon were both obscured.

Much disappointed, we began our return to camp. It was late and the clouds made the night very dark. For three hours we felt our way down the rocks with great care. Then we lost our way and dared proceed no farther. Rain came down in torrents and no shelter could be found. We could neither climb up nor go down and in the darkness dared not move about. So we sat and "weathered out" the night.

I wondered how the men fared.

August 8

Daylight came after a long—oh, how long!—night. We soon reached camp. After breakfast we were on the river again, then made two tiresome portages. The limestone of this canyon was polished and made beautiful marble. The rocks were of many colors: white, gray, pink, and purple, with saffron tints. We camped, after a hard portage, under an overhanging wall, glad to find shelter from the rain. A few sticks of driftwood made a fire, just enough to boil a cup of coffee.

August 9

The scenery was on a grand scale. The walls, twenty-five hundred feet high, were of marble, of many beautiful colors. I walked a mile on marble pavement, all polished and embossed in a thousand fantastic patterns. We named this Marble Canyon.

Riding down the river a short distance, we came upon a beautiful view: the river turned sharply and was enclosed by a wall set with a million brilliant gems.

What could it mean, everyone wondered?

Upon closer inspection, we found fountains of water bursting from the rocks. It was the water droplets reflecting the sunshine that formed the "gems." The rocks below the fountains were covered with mosses, green ferns, and beautiful flowering plants. We named it Vasey's Paradise, in honor of the botanist who traveled with me last year.

The river was quiet now, the canyon wider.

August 10

Walls still higher; the water swift again. At two o'clock we reached the mouth of the Little Colorado. It was a very small river and exceedingly muddy and salty.

The Howland brothers and Billy Dunn seemed extremely unhappy.

Down into the
Great Unknown

Our boats were riding high and buoyant, for
their loads were lighter than we would desire.
Only a month's rations remained. The flour had
been resifted. The few pounds of dried apples
had been spread in the sun and reshrunken to
their normal bulk. The sugar had all melted and
gone its way down the river. We had one large
sack of coffee.

The lightening of the boats had this advantage:
they would ride the waves better, and we would
have but little to carry when making a portage.

We were now ready at last to start down the
Great Unknown, the unexplored part of the Grand
Canyon. We were three quarters of a mile in the
depths of the earth. Against the towering walls and
cliffs, everything shrank into insignificance. The
waves were but puny ripples, and we but Pygmies.

We had an unknown distance yet to run, an unknown river to explore. What falls were there we knew not. What rocks beset the channel we knew not. What walls rose over the river we knew not. Ah, well! We may guess many things. Most of the men talked as cheerfully as ever. Jests were bandied about freely this morning. But to me the cheer was somber and the jests ghastly.

With eagerness and anxiety and misgiving, we entered the canyon and were carried along by the swift water through walls that rose from its very edge. We ran six miles in half an hour, then made a portage. On we went, gliding by hills and ledges, sweeping past sharp angles of rock, until we had made another five miles, when we landed for dinner.

Our meal concluded, we let down lines over a long rapid and started again. We proceeded with great care and constant watchfulness, making but four miles this afternoon.

Tonight we camped in a cave.

August 14

We could see but a little way into the granite gorge down which we must travel, but what we saw looked threatening. After breakfast we entered on the waves. At the very introduction the gorge inspired awe. The passage was narrower than any we had ever before experienced. The water was swifter. The walls were set with pinnacles and crags.

We heard a great roar ahead and approached it cautiously. The sound grew louder and louder. Soon we found ourselves above a long, broken fall, with rocks obstructing the river. The rushing waters crashed into great waves, lashing themselves into a mad, white foam. We could land just above the falls, but there was no foothold on either side by which we could make a portage. It was nearly a thousand feet to the top of the granite gorge, so it would have been impossible to carry our boats around.

There was no hesitation. Away we went, first on smooth, swift water. Then we struck a glassy wave and rode to its top, down again into the trough, up again on a higher wave, and down and up on waves higher and still higher. Suddenly, we struck a wave just as it was curling back, and the breaker rolled into my boat.

Still on we sped, shooting past rocks, until the *Emma Dean* was caught in a whirlpool and spun

SUDDENLY, WE STRUCK A WAVE JUST AS IT WAS CURLING BACK, AND THE BREAKER ROLLED INTO MY BOAT.

round. *The Maid* and *Kitty Clyde's Sister* passed us by. We drifted down another hundred yards through breakers—how we scarcely knew. The other boats were waiting to catch us as we came, for the men had seen our boat was almost swamped. The *Emma Dean* was bailed out, and on we went.

The walls were now more than a mile in height—a vertical distance difficult to appreciate. If you stood on the south steps of the Treasury Building in Washington, D.C., and looked down Pennsylvania Avenue to the Capitol, that is a little over one mile. Picture this distance overhead, and imagine cliffs extending to that altitude, and you will understand what a great depth we were in.

This gorge was black and narrow. Down into these grand, gloomy depths we glided, ever listening for falls, as the mad waters kept up their roar. We were constantly peering ahead, for the narrow canyon was winding and the river was closed in. We could see but a few hundred yards. What dangers lay below we knew not.

At last we camped on a narrow bench for the night. It rained hard, and we had no shelter. With a few sticks lodged in the rocks, Hawkins kindled a fire and cooked our supper. We sat on the rocks all night, wrapped in our ponchos, getting what sleep we could.

August 15

In the morning we studied the river. The waters reeled and rolled and boiled. We threw in sticks of driftwood to see where we must steer so that we could pass through in safety. We were scarcely able to determine where to go.

We set off. My boat was carried to the right, close to a wall. Then she was shot into the stream and dragged to the other side, where, caught in a whirlpool, she spun about like a mad top.

We could neither land nor run as we pleased. All three boats were entirely unmanageable. No order in their running could be preserved. First the *Emma Dean* was in front, then *Maid of the Canyon* was ahead, then *Kitty Clyde's Sister*. Each crew labored for its own preservation.

In such a place we came to another rapid. Two of the boats ran it. One succeeded in landing, but there was no foothold by which to make a portage so she was pushed out again into the stream. The next minute a great wave filled the open compartment. She was waterlogged. Breaker after breaker rolled over her until one capsized her.

The men were thrown out, but they clung to the boat. She drifted some distance alongside us until we were able to catch her.

To add to our misery it rained! Rills formed in the cliffs above. These grew into brooks. The brooks grew into creeks and tumbled over the walls in innumerable cascades, adding their wild music to the roar of the river.

August 16

We dried our rations again today and made new oars. The Colorado River, never a clear stream, was now exceedingly turbid. For the past three days it had been raining much of the time, and the floods pouring over the walls had brought down great quantities of mud.

The men seemed disgruntled. I blamed them not. We must proceed with haste.

August 17

In checking our food, I found our few rations

spoiled even more. We now had only musty flour sufficient for ten days and a few dried apples, but still plenty of coffee.

We must make all haste possible! I thought. If we were to meet with more difficulties, we would be compelled to give up the expedition and try to reach the Mormon settlements. I could only hope that the worst places were passed, but I knew not how much descent the river had yet to make.

I calculated over one hundred miles. But with so many twists to the river, my figure must have been off by any number of miles.

We made slow progress today, despite our desire to hurry. We ran with great caution, lest by another accident we were to lose our remaining supplies. How precious that little flour had become! We divided it among the boats and carefully stored it away, so it could be lost only by the loss of the boats themselves.

We made ten miles and camped among the rocks. We had rain from time to time all day and were thoroughly drenched and chilled. More than half the party were without hats. Not one of us had an entire suit of clothes, and we had not one blanket apiece.

We gathered driftwood and built a fire. But

The Mormons

The Mormons are a religious group, members of the Church of Jesus Christ of Latter-day Saints. In the first part of the nineteenth century they were often persecuted in the East and Midwest. In 1847 many Mormons followed their leader, Brigham Young, west to Utah. There they founded Salt Lake City. Other Mormons built settlements throughout Utah, wherever they could find sufficient water for their farms and outposts.

The Mormon explorer Jacob Hamblin discovered a way to cross the Colorado River at Lee's Ferry, Arizona. He also found another crossing farther downstream at the Grand Wash Cliffs. It was here that Powell's expedition finally left the depths of the Grand Canyon.

after supper the rain, coming down in torrents, extinguished it. We sat up all night on the rocks, shivering, and were more exhausted by the night's discomfort than by the day's toil.

August 19

Rain again this morning. We were in our granite prison still. The time until noon was occupied in making a long, bad portage.

After dinner, in running a rapid, the *Emma Dean* was upset by a wave. The river was rough and swift, and we were unable to land. The men in the boats behind saw our trouble, but they were caught in whirlpools and were spinning in eddies. A long time passed before they came to our relief.

We found a beach with just enough room to land. Here we camped, but there was no wood. Across the river we saw some driftwood lodged in the rocks. We brought two boatloads over, built a huge fire, and spread everything to dry. It was the first cheerful night we had had for a week.

August 20

We ran ten miles and discovered more Indian ruins. This was evidently quite a village. In one place there were many beautiful flint chips, as if this had been the home of an old arrow maker.

The Indians must have lived here deep in the

canyon, hiding from their enemies. I wonder how they found their way here. The men must wonder, too. If we but find their trail, is this a place to escape from the canyon?

August 21

We started early, cheered by the prospect of a fine day and encouraged by the good run yesterday. From around a curve came a mad roar, and down we were carried with a dizzying velocity to the head of another rapid. I stood on deck, supporting myself with a strap fastened on either side of the gunwale. The boat glided rapidly where the water was smooth, then, striking a wave, she leapt and bounded like a thing of life. We had a wild, exhilarating ride for ten miles, which we made in less than an hour.

The excitement was so great we forgot the danger until we heard the roar of a great fall below. We backed our oars and made another portage.

Here we were out of the dreaded granite prison!

Good cheer returned. We forgot the storms and the gloom and the cloud-covered canyons and the black granite and the raging river, and pushed our boats from shore in great glee.

August 22

We came to rapids this morning, let the boats down nearly half a mile, and made a long portage. We made seven miles today. Unfortunately, part of our flour was soaked in the river again.

August 23

Our way was through marble walls. We made fine progress, carried along by a swift river, shooting over rapids and finding no serious obstructions. We camped in a marble cave. We had run twenty-two miles.

August 24

The canyon was wider today. The walls rose three thousand feet. We ran twenty miles. How anxious we were to get out of this dreaded canyon, now that our diet was confined to coffee, a little spoiled flour for baking biscuits, and a few dried apples!

Our expedition became a race for dinner. Would we leave the canyon before our food ran out?

We made such fine progress today that all

hands were in good cheer, and not a moment of daylight was lost.

Around our fire tonight I looked at the weary, sunburned men in their tattered clothes. They appeared so different from those who began our journey but three months ago.

August 25

Thirty-five miles today. Hurrah!

Our Party Separates

We discovered an Indian garden. The Indians had planted corn, which was not yet ripe. There were some nice green squashes. We carried a dozen onboard our boats and hurriedly left. We were not willing to be caught in the robbery, excusing our theft by pleading our great want.

We ran a short distance to where we felt certain no Indian could follow and then we stopped to cook the squashes. What a kettle we made! Never was fruit so sweet as those stolen squashes.

When we stopped, just at dusk, we found we had run thirty-five miles again. A few more days like this and we would be out!

We had a royal supper—bread from some of our remaining flour, green squash sauce, and strong coffee. We had been for days on half rations, but now had no stint of roast squash.

THE BLADE OF ONE OAR WAS PUSHED INTO A LITTLE CREVICE IN SUCH A MANNER THAT IT HELD ME PRESSED AGAINST THE WALL.

We came to a place in the river much worse than any we had yet met. We landed but saw no way to let the boats down. To run the river would be sure destruction.

In my eagerness to reach a point where I could see the roaring fall below, I went too far up the rock wall. I could neither advance nor retreat. I stood with one foot on a projecting rock and clung with my hand fixed in a little crevice. Finding I was caught here, suspended four hundred feet above the river, I called for help.

The men passed me a line, but I could not let go of the rock long enough to take hold of it. They said they would bring the two largest oars. All of this took time, which seemed very precious to me. At last the men arrived.

The blade of one oar was pushed into a little crevice in such a manner that it held me pressed against the wall. The other oar was fixed so I could step on it.

Thus I was saved again.

I had seen that below the first roaring fall there was a second fall, but how great I could not tell. Below that was a rapid, filled with huge rocks for two hundred yards. I told the men we were to run it in the morning.

After supper Seneca Howland asked to talk with me. He thought we had better abandon the river here. I learned that he, his brother Oramel, and Billy Dunn had decided to go no farther in the boats.

I showed him on my map where I supposed we were, and where several Mormon settlements were.

We had a short talk and he lay down to sleep. But for me there was no sleep. All night long I paced.

Was it wise to go on? I felt we could get over the danger immediately before us. What lay below that I knew not.

Also, I was not sure we could climb out of the canyon here. And even if we could, a desert of rock and sand separated us from the nearest Mormon town, seventy-five miles away. Where would we find drinking water if we were to leave?

I almost decided to abandon the expedition. But for years I had contemplated this trip. To leave the exploration unfinished, to say there was a part of the Grand Canyon I could not explore, having nearly accomplished it, was more than I was willing to acknowledge.

I determined to go on.

I woke my brother and told him of Howland's decision. Walter promised to stay with me. I called up Hawkins and he made a like promise. Sumner, Bradley, and Hall all agreed to go on with us.

August 28

We breakfasted without a word being said about the future. The meal was as solemn as a funeral.

I asked the three men if they still thought it was best to leave. The older Howland thought it was. Dunn agreed with him. The younger Howland tried to persuade them to go on with us. Failing in that, he decided to go with his brother.

With the loss of hands, we would not be able to run all the boats. I decided to leave behind my *Emma Dean*. Battered as she was, she had served us well.

Two rifles and a shotgun were given to the men climbing out. I asked them to help themselves to the rations and take what they thought to be a fair share. This they refused to do, saying they could shoot something to eat.

Before returning to the river, we took out our barometers, fossils, minerals, and ammunition and left them on the rocks. We were going over this place as lightly as possible.

The last thing before leaving, I wrote a letter to my wife and gave it to Seneca Howland. Sumner gave him his watch, asking that it be sent to his sister should he not be heard from again. The records of the expedition had been kept in duplicate and one set was given to Howland, too.

Now we were ready to start.

For the last time our three comrades begged us not to go on. They told us it was madness to continue in this place. Tears were shed. It was a solemn parting, each party thinking the other was taking the more dangerous course.

I named this Separation Rapids.

I boarded the *Maid of the Canyon* with my brother and Jack Sumner. Hall, Bradley, and Hawkins rode in the *Kitty Clyde's Sister*. Captain Howland, his younger brother, and Billy Dunn watched us set off.

The *Maid of the Canyon* glided rapidly along the foot of the wall, grazed a great rock, pulled into the chute of the second fall and plunged over it.

The crewmen pulled with all their power and swung clear of the dangerous rocks below.

We were scarcely a minute in running the rapid, and found that, although it looked bad from above, we had passed many places that were worse!

Kitty Clyde's Sister followed us shortly. We quickly landed and fired our guns as a signal to our companions above that we had come over in safety. Then we remained a couple of hours, hoping they would take the *Emma Dean* and follow us. We waited until it seemed hopeless and then pushed on.

In the late afternoon we camped on a narrow rock. Where did the Howlands and Dunn sleep this evening?

Success!

We started early this morning. The river continued swift, but we had no serious difficulty. Then, at 12 o'clock, the walls suddenly opened up. The river rolled wide and beautiful before us. We had reached the Grand Wash, the end of the canyon.

We had emerged from the Grand Canyon of the Colorado!

The relief from danger and the joy of success were great. Ever before us had been the unknown. Nearly every waking hour passed in the Grand Canyon had been one of toil, hardship, and hunger. We had watched the disappearance of our scant supply of rations. We had endured those gloomy depths, where clouds hid the sky by day and only a narrow zone of stars could be seen at night. But now the danger was over, the toil had ceased, the gloom had disappeared!

This night we camped on the left bank in a

mesquite thicket. The river rolled by us in silent majesty. The quiet of camp was sweet after the incessant roar of the river. Our joy was almost ecstasy.

We sat until long after midnight, talking of our adventures and of home but mostly of the three friends who had left us. Were they wandering in those depths, unable to find a way out? Were they searching for water over the desert lands above? Or were they nearing the Mormon settlements?

Tomorrow should bring us to a settlement ourselves.

August 30

Today we ran three short, low canyons. We pushed on with some urgency for we knew we were near the mouth of the Virgin River.

In the afternoon we saw four strange men on the shore and pulled toward them. They recognized us!

As we talked we learned that they were far less surprised to see us than we were to see them. They said we had been reported lost long ago. They were watching for any fragments of our party that might drift down the stream.

How high our hopes had been when we had departed the Green River settlement so long ago in May. Ten men, four boats, ten months of supplies, and my blank map to fill in.

With me now were five men and two boats. Our supplies had dwindled to ten pounds of flour, fifteen pounds of dried apples, and eighty pounds of coffee.

But we had conquered the Grand Canyon!

However, before I share my tale with my countrymen, I must learn what fate befell my departed men.

I will begin this search on the morrow.

NOW THE DANGER WAS OVER, THE TOIL HAD CEASED, THE GLOOM HAD DISAPPEARED. WE HAD CONQUERED THE GRAND CANYON!

EPILOGUE

No one knows for sure what happened to Seneca and Oramel Howland and William Dunn, the three men who left the expedition in its final days. Powell searched for them. Leaders of the Mormon Church sent riders to the various ranches and Indian villages of the region, but no word came back. Although eager to return home, Powell waited and waited. Finally, he could wait no longer and started for home.

Two days into his journey, Powell heard a story about his lost companions. It seems that Dunn and the Howlands had climbed out of the canyon only to die at the hands of a band of Shivwits Indians. Apparently, the white men had insulted the Native Americans, an act that ended in their deaths somewhere on the lonely rim of the Grand Canyon. To this day, however, there is no proof that this was indeed the fate of the three hardy explorers.

Major Powell, riding in a luxurious railroad palace car as he headed east, was treated to a hero's welcome everywhere he went. He chuckled as he read the newspaper reports of his supposed death.

Later, he made speeches in Salt Lake City, Detroit, Cincinnati, Chicago, and at home in Normal, Illinois. He was considered a national hero and was invited to Washington, D.C.

Through his vision and force of will, John Wesley Powell filled in the last blank space on the map of the American West. The names he gave to the rapids and canyons—Ashley, Echo, Lodore, Cataract, Glen, Marble, Separation, and dozens more—remind us of the challenges he and his companions faced.

Powell went on to lead more expeditions down the Colorado. Many of the places he explored have disappeared forever, flooded by the dams built at Glen Canyon and Flaming Gorge. Only through his words can we visit these lost sites today.

Yet much of what Powell saw and experienced is still enjoyed by those who follow his pioneering trail in rafts and wooden boats down the Colorado and through the Grand Canyon.

EDITORS' NOTE

As he explored the Grand Canyon, John Wesley Powell wrote in his journal every chance he could. The purpose of his notes, as he later said, was not to tell a story but to record scientific data: "The exploration was not made for adventure, but purely for scientific purposes, geographic and geologic. I had no intention of writing an account of it, but only of recording scientific results."

But the American people desired to know more than just the "scientific results." They wanted to hear the dramatic story of the expedition. So Powell revised and expanded his journal into a book, *The Exploration of the Colorado River and Its Canyons*. This is the main text upon which we have based our work.

Powell's writing style was often confusing and his sentences rather lengthy. To help clarify his story and to make the book more pleasurable to read, we sometimes shortened sentences or left out repetitive passages. Also, he wrote in both the present and past tense. We chose to use the past tense throughout.

Wherever we edited Powell's words, we were careful to keep their meaning. Our aim has been to describe as faithfully as possible the exciting adventures of this remarkable man and his brave companions.

Following are the works that we have consulted:

Jenkinson, Michael. *Wild Rivers of North America.* New York: Dutton, 1973.

Powell, John Wesley. *Down the Colorado.* Photographs by Eliot Porter. New York: Dutton, 1969.

Powell, John Wesley. *The Exploration of the Colorado River and Its Canyons.* New York: Dover, 1961.

Stegner, Wallace. *Beyond the Hundredth Meridian.* Boston: Houghton Mifflin, 1954.

GLOSSARY

adobe sun-dried mud molded into blocks for building

alcove a narrow opening into a canyon wall

altitude height above sea level

amphitheater curved area surrounded by slanting rock (like an outdoor theater or stadium)

arch curved opening of rock

botanist a person who studies plants

broadside sideways

butte a steep hill with a flat top

canyon a deep narrow valley with steep sides, often with a stream flowing through it

capsize overturn

cataract a very large steep waterfall

channel the bed of a river; the passageway for a boat shooting the rapids

chute a narrow, angled passage between rocks

conflagration a large fire

crag a steep jagged rock or cliff

crevice a narrow opening in a rock or rock wall

crimson a deep purple-red color

disgruntled unhappy; discontented; ill-humored

effects movable property

etch to carve; an etching is a carving

exhilarating exciting, lively, stimulating

geologist a person who studies rocks, mountains, and cliffs to find out what the earth is made of and what changes have taken place over the years

glen a small narrow valley

gorge a narrow passage through land; a steep-walled canyon or part of a canyon

gulch a narrow valley with steep sides

labyrinth a place full of intricate passageways

latitude distance measured on the earth's surface north and south of the equator

lichened covered with lichens; a lichen is a special organism made up of a kind of algae and a fungus; lichens grow on rocks

longitude distance measured on the earth's surface east and west of an imaginary line passing through the town of Greenwich, England

plateau an area of flat land that is raised above the surrounding country

portage (POOR tij) to carry a boat and equipment overland around an obstacle such as rapids

portal an entrance

precipice (PREH suh puhs) edge of a high, steep overhanging of rock

rapids a rocky part of a river where the water flows very fast

ration a fixed portion or share of food

rill a very small brook

roseate (ROH zee uht) a pink-to-light-rose color

saffron a yellow-orange color

solemn serious; awe-inspiring

terrace a raised bank of earth with a flat top and sloping sides

turbid muddy

vermilion (vuhr MIL yuhn) a bright reddish orange color

TO LEARN MORE ABOUT JOHN WESLEY POWELL AND THE GRAND CANYON

FOR FURTHER READING

Anderson, Peter. *A Grand Canyon Journey.* New York: Franklin Watts, 1997.

Fraser, Mary Ann. *In Search of the Grand Canyon.* New York: Henry Holt, 1995.

Miller, Peter. "John Wesley Powell: Vision for the West." *National Geographic Magazine* (April 1994): 86–115.

Rawlings, Carol. *Grand Canyon.* Austin, TX: Raintree, Steck-Vaughn, 1995.

Vieira, Linda, and Christopher Canyon. *Grand Canyon, a Trail Through Time.* New York: Walker and Company, 1997.

VIDEOS

River of Stone: The Powell Expedition. Salt Lake City: Bonneville Worldwide Entertainment, 1997.

PLACES TO VISIT

Amerind Foundation Museum
P.O. Box 400
Dragoon, AZ 85609
520-586-3666

Canyon de Chelly National Monument
  P.O. Box 588
  Chinle, AZ 86503
Canyonlands National Park
  2282 SW Resource Blvd.
  Moab, UT 84532
Glen Canyon National Recreation Area
  P.O. Box 1507
  Page, AZ 86040
Grand Canyon National Park
  P.O. Box 129
  Grand Canyon, AZ 86023

For information about visiting Native American reservations, please contact the Native American Travel Service at 602-945-0771.

WEBSITES*

www.grand-canyon.az.us/grand.htm.
  Excellent site for maps and information about the Grand Canyon.
www.nps.gov/grca.
  This is the official site of the National Park Service, with maps, trails, and photos.
www.azstarbet.cin/grandcanyonriver.
  Fun site with a virtual raft trip down the Colorado River through the Grand Canyon.

*Websites change from time to time. For additional on-line information, check with the media specialist at your local library.

INDEX

Page numbers for illustrations are in boldface